MILITARY ENGINEERING
☆ ☆ ☆
IN ACTION

MISSILES

SELF-GUIDED EXPLOSIVES

Earle Rice Jr.

Enslow Publishing
101 W. 23rd Street
Suite 240
New York, NY 10011
USA
enslow.com

Published in 2017 by Enslow Publishing, LLC.

101 W. 23rd Street, Suite 240, New York, NY 10011

Copyright © 2017 by Enslow Publishing, LLC.

Library of Congress Cataloging-in-Publication Data

Names: Rice, Earle, author.
Title: Missiles : self-guided explosives / Earle Rice Jr.
Description: New York, NY : Enslow Publishing, [2017] | Series: Military engineering in action | Includes bibliographical references and index.
Identifiers: LCCN 2015045449| ISBN 9780766075245 (library bound) | ISBN 9780766075214 (pbk.) | ISBN 9780766075238 (6-pack)
Subjects: LCSH: Guided missiles—Juvenile literature. | Ballistic missiles—Juvenile literature.
Classification: LCC UG1310 .R53 2016 | DDC 358.1/7182—dc23
LC record available at http://lccn.loc.gov/2015045449

Printed in the United States of America

To Our Readers: We have done our best to make sure all website addresses in this book were active and appropriate when we went to press. However, the author and the publisher have no control over and assume no liability for the material available on those websites or on any websites they may link to. Any comments or suggestions can be sent by e-mail to customerservice@enslow.com.

Photos Credits: Cover, p. 1 Dejan Lazarevic/Shutterstock.com (missiles in foreground, p. 2), © iStockphoto. com/Alex Potemkin (missiles in background); art/background throughout Dianka Pyzhova/Shutterstock. com, Ensuper/Shutterstock.com, foxie/Shutterstock.com, kasha_malasha/Shutterstock.com, pashabop/Shutterstock.com; p. 4 dikobraziy/Shutterstock.com; p. 6 U.S. Air Force/432nd Wing/432nd Air Expeditionary Wing; p. 8 U.S. Air Force/Senior Airman BreeAnn Sachs; p. 9 Universal History Archive/UIG/Getty Images; p. 10 NASA/Marshall Space Flight Center/Getty Images; p. 12 OFF/AFP/Getty Images; p. 13 U.S. Navy/Petty Officer 3rd Class Jonathan Sunderman; p. 14 NASA; p. 15 Michael Peterson/DVIDS; p. 19 U.S. Navy/Intelligence Specialist 1st Class Kenneth Moll./Wikimedia Commons/USS_Cape_St._George_%28CG_71%29_fires_a_ tomahawk_missile_in_support_of_OIF.jpg/public domain; p. 20 U.S. Navy/Mass Communication Specialist 3rd Class Justin R. DiNiro/Released; p. 25 U.S. Navy/Mass Communication Specialist 2nd Class Daniel M. Young/Released; p. 26 Airman Magazine/MSgt Dave Nolan/WikimediaCommons/MH-53J Pave Low III. jpg/public domain; p. 31 U.S. Air Force/Master Sgt. John H. DeGroot/Wikimedia Commons/File:B-1 bomb loading.jpg/public domain; p. 33 Eugene Berman/Shutterstock.com; p. 35 U.S. Navy/Mass Communication Specialist 2nd Class Jacob G. Sisco/Wikimedia Commons/ File:USS Carl Vinson (CVN 70) 141204-N-ZP059- 040 (15949151931).jpg/public domain; p. 38 U.S. Air Force/Beau Wade; p. 39 U.S. Air Force/Joe Davila; p. 42 U.S. Air Force/Michael Peterson; p. 43 STAFF SGT. ALAN R. WYCHECK/Wikimedia Commons/ File:Minuteman III in silo 1989.jpg/public domain.

CONTENTS

US Air Force personnel stationed in the United States can operate an unmanned Predator drone in countries across the globe, including Afghanistan.

Hellfire and Predators: A New Kind of Warfare

It was a new kind of warfare. Airman First Class Brandon Bryant was one of its pioneers. He did not fly a jet fighter, carry a pack and a rifle, or ever set foot on a battlefield. In 2007, Bryant reported for duty in a windowless metal box at Nellis Air Force Base (AFB), a sprawling stretch of tarmac and maintenance hangars outside Las Vegas. The box he worked in was dark and cold—exactly 68 degrees Fahrenheit (20 degrees Celsius)—in deference to the computer equipment that served as his weapons. He sat in a padded cockpit chair, staring at a computer screen. The darkness helped him to focus on controlling the MQ-1B Predators circling 2 miles (3.2 kilometers) above the rough Afghan countryside.

An MQ-1B Predator is a remotely piloted aircraft that can perform intelligence, surveillance and reconnaissance, close-air support, combat search and rescue, and precision strike missions.

Brandon Bryant acted as the eyes of the Predator. He focused an array of cameras and aimed its targeting laser. Bryant worked in tandem with the Predator's pilot, seated next to him. Launching a Hellfire missile was a joint operation: the pilot pulled a trigger, and Bryant directed the high-explosive warhead by laser to its desired objective. Both the pilot and Bryant were a new kind of warrior called drone operators.

On Bryant's console, the image of the midwinter landscape of Afghanistan's Kunar Province appeared. His eyes scanned a palette of browns and grays, stubbled fields, and dark forests making their way up the rocky foothills of the Hindi Kush. He zoomed the camera in on two suspected insurgents. Each wore traditional *shalwar kameez* (pantaloons and body shirt). He knew nothing about them. They were nonentities to Bryant. A directive from someone up the mysterious chain of command that led to his headset told him they would be carrying rifles. He switched from the visible spectrum—the view of browns and grays—to the sharply contrasting infrared. The heat signatures of the insurgents appeared ghostly white against the cool dark earth.

A safety observer stood behind Bryant to ensure the weapon release procedure was properly executed. The observer recited a long verbal checklist, while Bryant targeted his laser on the two insurgents. A countdown—three, two, one—then the flat command "missile off the rail." Seventy-five hundred miles (12,070 km) away, a Predator's Hellfire missile fired up, shot from its attachment, and streaked to supersonic speed in seconds. The atmosphere in the cold Nevada box fell deathly silent except for the whir of electronic machinery. Bryant and the others entered temporarily into a kind of timeless limbo, straining to stay focused on the white-hot clarity of the infrared. Then, suddenly, the silent screen lit up in a dazzling white glare. Bryant continued to stare at the monitor until its obscene image became indelibly imprinted in his memory like an etching on a copper plate.

In US Air Force parlance, Brandon Bryant was a remotely piloted aircraft sensor operator, or simply a "sensor." He belonged to a US Air Force squadron that flew MQ-1 Predator drones over the battlegrounds of Iraq and Afghanistan. Barely weeks beyond his twenty-first birthday, this had been Brandon's first wartime operation. He was a twenty-first-century warrior in a new kind of combat.

Unmanned Aircraft Systems Operator

Many drones are used by the US Army for reconnaissance. Unmanned aircraft systems operators are remote pilots of unmanned observation aircrafts that gather intelligence used in operational tactics. As intelligence specialists, they are integral to providing army personnel with information about enemy forces and battle areas.

Their duties include air reconnaissance, surveillance, targeting, and acquisition missions. Operators plan and analyze flight missions and perform preflight, in-flight, and post-flight checks and procedures. They launch and recover airframes from the runway and perform maintenance on various types of equipment.

Student sensor operators practice tactical operations during an MQ-1 Predator simulator mission.

First Ballistic Missile

The V-2 (Vergeltungswaffe Zwei, or "Vengeance Weapon Two") claims distinction as the world's first operational ballistic missile. A ballistic missile is one type of rocket that carries warheads to a specific target. Beginning in 1936, it was developed by a team of German scientists led by Wernher von Braun at Peenemünde, an island in the North Sea. It was first launched against Great Britain on September 8, 1944.

The V-2 measured 47 feet (14 meters) long and weighed 28,000–29,000 pounds (12,701–13,154 kilograms). Its single-chamber rocket motor burned alcohol and liquid oxygen and developed about 60,000 pounds (27,216 kg) of thrust. The V-2 carried a payload of 1,600 pounds (726 kg) of high explosives. It reached a height of almost 50 miles (80 km) and a range of about 200 miles (320 km).

A. Bowdoin Van Riper, writing in *Rockets and Missiles*, tallied the damage inflicted by the V-1 and V-2 missiles. Together, they destroyed 33,700 buildings and damaged 204,000, while killing 12,685 people and injuring 26,433.

The United States tests a captured German V-2 rocket in 1946. At the end of the war, a race began between the United States and Russia to retrieve as many V-2 rockets and personnel as possible.

Dr. Wernher von Braun stands next to F-1 engines of the Saturn V rocket.

The Origins of Drones

The idea of unmanned airborne messengers of death is not really new. Some analysts trace the origins of drones back to the German V-1 and V-2 rockets launched against Great Britain during World War II. The V-1 ("V" for Vergeltungswaffe or "Vengeance Weapon") was called a "flying bomb." It was actually an early cruise missile. Its successor, the V-2, was a much advanced improvement. Together, they rained terror down upon Britons for more than nine months in 1944 and 1945.

In early 1945, as the Soviet army advanced toward Germany, von Braun and his team of scientists fled Peenemünde. They all went into hiding until they could surrender willingly to American troops. In a remarkable turn of events, von Braun signed a contract with the US government. The Americans flew him to the United States, where he began a new chapter in his life.

Dawn of the Missile Age: Strategic Missile Force

At the end of World War II, the United States and the Soviet Union (USSR) entered into a missile development race. The intense rivalry of the two nations formed a part of what was to become known as the Cold War.

Both the United States and the Soviet Union imported German scientists who had helped to develop the V-2 rocket. Wernher von Braun and his V-2 team were brought to the United States under Operation Paperclip. The US government, reported Thomas Parrish in *The Cold War Encyclopedia*, contracted von Braun to "undertake such research, design, development, and other tasks associated with jet propulsion and guided missiles" as might be directed. The aim of both nations was to produce strategic ballistic missiles more effective than the other for the delivery of nuclear warheads.

William Picketing, James Van Allen, and Wernher von Braun brandish a model of the first American satellite, *Explorer I*, after the satellite was launched. This event signaled the birth of America's space program.

Developers of the first American and Soviet ballistic missiles used the V-2 as a starting point but steadily incorporated refinements. The Soviets produced a range of missiles designated R-1 through R-5. Introduced in 1956, the R-5 was the last of the line based on the V-2. It had a range of 700 miles (1,127 km) and carried a payload of 3,000 pounds (1,361 kg).

Meanwhile, von Braun and his team developed the Redstone missile. More powerful and more accurate than the V-2, it could deliver a 7,000-pound (3,175-kg) warhead on target within a radius of 1,000 feet (305 m). At the same time, the US developed a compact,

Types of Guided Missiles

Guided missiles are guided while they are in flight. There are three basic types:

- **Conventional Guided Missiles:** Air-to-air missile, air-to-surface missile, antiballistic missile, antisatellite weapon, antiship missile, antitank guided missile, surface-to-air missile, and wire-guided missile
- **Cruise Missiles**
- **Ballistic Missiles:** Intermediate-range ballistic missile, intercontinental ballistic missile, submarine-launched ballistic missile, theater ballistic missile, and tactical ballistic missile

A Tomahawk cruise missile is launched from the bow of the destroyer USS *Barry*.

The Redstone ballistic missile was a high-accuracy, liquid-propelled, surface-to-surface missile developed by the Army Ballistic Missile Agency, Redstone Arsenal, in Huntsville, Alabama, under the direction of Dr. von Braun. The Redstone rocket was also known as "Old Reliable" because of its many diverse missions.

lightweight nuclear bomb. Combining the two, the Redstone became the world's first missile capable of delivering a nuclear bomb. Together, the Soviet R-5M and the Redstone formed the dividing line between the first and second generations of ballistic missiles.

Birth of the ICBM

The second generation of ballistic missiles began in August 1957. The Soviets announced the first successful launch of the R-7. Nicknamed the Semyorka (or "Seven"), it was the world's first intercontinental ballistic missile (ICBM). The R-7 was liquid-fueled, had a range of 3,000 miles (4,828 km), and carried a payload of 12,000 pounds (5,443 kg). The Semyorka was the forerunner of the long-lived Soyuz line of launch vehicles.

In October 1957, the Soviets shocked the world with the launch of *Sputnik I*, the first artificial Earth-orbiting satellite. The Americans matched the Soviet achievement when the Redstone missile launched the *Explorer I* satellite in January 1958.

First Lieutenant Kira Gonzalez, Missile Combat Crew commander, runs through missile procedures at Vandenberg Air Force Base in preparation for the launch of an unarmed Minuteman III intercontinental ballistic missile.

To keep pace with the Soviet missilery advances, the United States accelerated work on the Atlas—America's first ICBM—in March 1954 and began work on an alternate missile named Titan in May 1955. Both missiles were powered with liquid-fueled engines. The first successful Atlas launch occurred at Cape Canaveral in December 1957. Titan I took to the air fourteen months later in February 1959. Their operational lifespans soon gave way to the Titan II and Minuteman I in the early 1960s.

Minuteman I was the first American ICBM to use solid rather than liquid fuel. By 1965, the US had retired all Atlas and Titan I missiles. Titan II and Minuteman I became the mainstay of America's strategic missile force. (Land-based heavy bombers—B-2 and B-52—and submarine-launched ballistic missiles (SLBMs)—currently the Trident II—form the other two arms of the US strategic nuclear triad.) By 1974, all Minuteman I missiles were replaced by either Minuteman II or Minuteman III missiles. The air force deactivated Titan II in 1982.

Today's nuclear triad consists of Trident II SLBMs on 14 ballistic missile submarines, each carrying up to 24 missiles, 450 Minuteman III ICBMs (see chapter 6), and about 60 B-2 and B-52 bombers. Plans are underway to replace aging elements of this triad.

For a time, Americans enjoyed a superior nuclear force, but the Soviets soon achieved nuclear equality. A new race to develop an antiballistic missile (ABM) began. Toward the end of the Kennedy administration in the early 1960s, American strategists adopted a defense doctrine called Mutually Assured Destruction (MAD). The thinking behind MAD was that no nuclear power would attack another knowing that it would mean certain death to both the attacked and the attacker.

In October 1962, a high-flying US U-2F aircraft spotted a Soviet ballistic missile on a launch pad in western Cuba. President John F. Kennedy placed a naval blockade around the island and confronted the Soviets. The world stood on the brink of a nuclear war. After thirteen terrifying days, Soviet premier Nikita Khrushchev—in a

Essential Elements of a Guided Missile

Warhead
The warhead contains either a high explosive or a nuclear device and a fusing system. A fusing system sets off a small charge that triggers the main explosion.

Engine
Missiles are powered by either a rocket engine or a jet engine. A rocket engine produces thrust (forward motion) by expelling hot gases at extremely high speed. Combustion creates the hot gases that are ejected through a nozzle at the rear of the rocket. A jet engine operates similarly, except that it draws its air from the atmosphere.

Guidance and Control System
A guidance system usually consists of a computer and special instruments to establish the missile's course. It sends electronic signals to a system of movable devices— fins, vanes, and wings—that control flight.

secret agreement revealed later—agreed to remove Soviet missiles from Cuba. In return, the US agreed to remove US missiles from Turkey and not to invade Cuba. The confrontation led to the Nuclear Test Ban Treaty in August 1963.

CHAPTER 3

Cruise Missiles: Radar-Dodging Terrain Followers

At 0534 hours local time on March 20, 2003, a series of explosions shattered the early morning stillness of Baghdad. Huge clouds of smoke rose in the air, and the red glow of flames lit up the horizon. The blasts signaled the start of the "shock-and-awe" attack on the Iraqi capital by the United States and allied coalition forces at the outset of the Iraq War. It was spearheaded by some 320 Tomahawk cruise missiles launched from ships in the Red Sea and the Persian Gulf. The destruction they wrought was all but indescribable. Al Jazeera, the Arabic language television station, reported simply, "Baghdad is burning. What more can we say?"

A week later, in a windowless, sand-colored building in Bahrain, navy planners and "targeteers" stared at computer screens and prepared to launch a daily salvo of Tomahawks. The Fifth Fleet's Strike Center, where they worked, was surrounded by razor wire.

A Tomahawk Land Attack Missile (TLAM) is launched from the guided missile cruiser USS *Cape St. George* during Operation Iraqi Freedom.

A sign barred admittance to anyone without top-secret clearance. One of their targets was Saddam Hussein himself. "We tried to put one on his forehead last night," one officer told David S. Cloud, a staff reporter for the *Wall Street Journal*. By shifting residences, however, the Iraqi dictator eluded the cruise-missile marksmen.

Some Tomahawk targets were decided by the Pentagon weeks or even months earlier as part of the Iraq War plan. For those targets, navy planners spent hours of preparation. They had to examine satellite photos, plot coordinates, select routes, and choose the ships or submarines that would launch the missiles.

In other cases, a target of opportunity demanding fast action—such as Saddam Hussein—suddenly presented itself and set off a chain reaction. After intelligence gathering and evaluation in Washington, DC, the president authorized a missile strike. His decision was flashed electronically to the Strike Center in Bahrain. Officers there put together a target folder. Assessing the risk of civilian casualties, they decided how many missiles would be needed and which ships or submarines were best positioned to launch them. After alerting the air force to steer clear of missile flight paths, they were good to go.

Chief Sonar Technician Mark Strouse stands watch in the Combat Information Center (CIC) aboard the guided-missile cruiser USS *Normandy*.

When the strike officers are satisfied that all their preparations are ready, they flash orders by e-mail to ships operating in the Red Sea, Persian Gulf, or Mediterranean. On each ship, the communications center rushes a copy of the order to its combat information center. There, planners feed the essential codes into the vessel's computer system, triggering an alarm. The sound of the alarm clears the decks near the missile launch tubes. At the end of the chain, the ship's captain turns a key to activate the launch system, a launcher presses a button, and a missile lifts off with a roar and begins its deadly flight.

Meanwhile, for a seeming eternity, planners at the Strike Center continued to stare at their computers, oblivious to the destruction happening at the end of the chain. "It was surreal," an officer said to Cloud, "because it was no different than exercises we've practiced again and again. Hours later, you take a step back and see the video and see the hits coming in Baghdad and you realize it was real." In the first week of the Iraq War, the navy fired more than 800 cruise missiles.

Cruise Missile Development

Cruise missiles are so named because they generally operate at a cruising speed of 550 miles per hour (880 kilometers per hour). The Tomahawk takes its name from the Native American light war ax. Basically derived from the German V-1 and V-2 rockets of the World War II era, cruise missiles offer an alternative technology to ballistic missiles.

By the end of World War II, however, the United States had nineteen guided missile projects in progress. Many were based on the V-1 rocket. The 1970s gave rise to a new line of cruise missiles: the air-launched cruise missile or ALCM (pronounced al-cum), the ground-launched cruise missile or GLCM (glick-em), and the sea-launched cruise missile or SLCM (slick-em). The ever-reliable Tomahawk evolved from the SLCM. It later morphed into today's Tomahawk Land Attack Missile or TLAM. The TLAM is designed to hit stationary or moving targets on land.

Tomahawk Land Attack Missile (TLAM)

The Tomahawk is an all-weather, long-range, subsonic cruise missile. It is used for land-attack warfare and is launched from US Navy surface ships and US Navy and Royal Navy submarines.

General Characteristics

Primary Function: It is used to strike high-value or heavily defended land targets.

Contractor: Raytheon Systems Company

Length: 18 feet 3 inches (5.56 m)

Diameter: 20.4 inches (51.81 cm)

Weight: 2,650 pounds (1,202 kg)

Wingspan: 8 feet 9 inches (2.67 m)

Speed: Subsonic—about 550 mph (880 kmh)

Range: Block IV TLAM-E (latest variant)—900 nautical miles (1,000 statute miles; 1,600 km)

Guidance System: Block IV TLAM-E—Initial Navigation System (INS); Terrain Contour Matching (TERCOM); Digital Scene Matching Area Correlation (DSMAC); Global Positioning System (GPS)

Warhead: Block IV TLAM-E—Conventional submunitions dispenser with combined-effect bomblets

Basic Parts of a Cruise Missile

Cruise missiles generally consist of a guidance system, a propulsion system, and a payload. They are housed in an airframe with small wings and a tail assembly for flight control. The airframe of the Tomahawk Block IV, for example, is divided into five increments: nose, payload, mid-body, aft-body, and tail-cone sections.

Guidance System: A cruise missile uses one or more guidance systems:

- *Inertial Navigation System (INS)* uses stored data to follow a programmed route.
- *Global Positioning System (GPS)* transmits radio signals from twenty-four Earth-orbiting satellites giving the location of each satellite and the time of the transmission.
- *Terrain Contour Matching (TERCOM)* uses radar to detect and recognize landmarks as the missile flies over them.
- *Digital Scene Matching Aerial Correlation (DSMAC)* operates like TERCOM, but uses imagery, not radar.

Propulsion System: Cruise missiles are largely propelled by jet engines, preferring turbofan engines for their greater efficiency at low altitude and subsonic speed.

Payload: Conventional or nuclear warheads.

Conventional Guided Missiles: Offensive and Defensive

O n January 16, 1991, at 11 pm local time, four massive MH-53J Pave Low helicopters lifted off a chilly desert airfield in Saudi Arabia into a moonless night. Pilots of the 20th Special Operations Squadron could see their breath forming in foggy puffs in the cockpits of the MH-53J choppers. Right behind them, eight AH-64 Apache attack helicopters and a Blackhawk helicopter followed them into the pitch-black sky. Collectively, they formed Task Force Normandy, commanded by Lieutenant Colonel Dick Cody.

Their mission: Take out the Iraqi early warning network—all of it.

The Apaches and the Blackhawk belonged to the 101st Airborne Division. Troops of the Special Ops group were along as extra insurance in the event the choppers crashed or were shot down. The Blackhawk carried mechanics and spare parts. For the next

A Hellfire missile is launched from an MH-60S Sea Hawk helicopter.

two hours plus, they all skimmed along over the desert at sand-dune height toward the Iraqi early warning net and two designated targets. At preset coordinates, the group peeled off into two attack teams. The teams were ordered to maintain absolute radio silence until ten seconds before opening fire.

At 2:38 on the morning of January 17, 1991, the eight Apaches zeroed in on their targets and hovered low and unseen, 4 miles (6.4 km) south of the radars. Images of two Iraqi radar sites appeared on their forward-looking infrared screens. The sites were positioned just north of Saudi Arabia to detect intruding aircraft. They maintained constant communication with four Iraqi fighter bases, as well as a direct line to the Intelligence Operations Center in Baghdad.

MH-53J Pave Low helicopters were part of Task Force Normandy.

First Lieutenant Tom Drew, at the controls of Number 976 chopper, broke radio silence. "Party in ten," he said, as recounted by Richard Mackenzie in *Air Force Magazine*. Ten seconds later, on a prearranged cue, the Apaches fired off a volley of twenty-seven AGM-114 Hellfire air-to-ground missiles. "This one's for you, Saddam," growled Chief Warrant Officer 3 Dave Jones, at the controls of another Apache.

Their shots announced the start of Operation Desert Storm and touched off the Gulf War of 1991. They blinded Iraq's early warning net at a key moment. "If something had happened and we didn't do 100 percent [destruction]," recalled one gunner, Chief Warrant Officer 4 Lou Hall, "a lot of people were going to get hurt." Not to worry. They did their job—all of it.

Operation Normandy destroyed sixteen separate radar installations at each of two sites. Nothing but piles of twisted metal remained at the sites. And a 20-mile-wide (32-km) pathway was now open all the way to Baghdad.

Twenty-two minutes after the Apaches completed their lethal work, a flotilla of about one hundred allied aircraft arrived at Iraq's devastated portal and soared through the huge gap in the Iraqi surveillance network. Racing north, they dispensed similar destruction on critical, first-night targets in Baghdad. They found the city already under attack by US Air Force F-117 stealth fighter-bombers. The F-117s had used their stealth advantage to slip through Iraqi airspace without detection. They started their attack soon after the Apaches fired their opening rounds. But those who flew to Baghdad in unstealthy aircraft that night will remain forever grateful to the Apaches for making their flight easier.

When coalition commander General Norman Schwarzkopf heard the news back at the Central Command war room, he took a deep breath, clenched his jaw, and muttered, "Thank God!"

America's Missile Arsenal

America's arsenal of conventional guided missiles covers a broad spectrum of applications, both offensive and defensive. Missiles fall into three basic categories (see chapter 2). Variations increase the total to more than twenty.

One of the most widely used offensive missiles in the US inventory is the AGM-114 Hellfire. It is an air-to-surface missile originally designed as an antitank weapon. The Hellfire has a length of 5 feet, four inches (162.56 centimeters) and a diameter of 7 inches (17.77 cm), and carries a 16-pound (7.26-kg) high-explosive, shaped charge. Though generally fired from Apache or Super Cobra attack helicopters and Predator unmanned combat air vehicles, it can also be launched from fixed-wing aircraft, ships, and land-based systems.

In the Gulf War of 1991, US and Israeli Patriot batteries attempted to intercept forty-four extended-range SCUD missiles launched by Iraq against Israel and Saudi Arabia. American claims of success were eventually revised downward from a hit rate of 96 percent to 61 percent. Its record was still efficient enough for the Patriot to earn the nickname "Scudbuster." The latest version of the Patriot promises a far greater success rate.

Operation Desert Storm

In August 1990, Iraqi dictator Saddam Hussein ordered his army into Kuwait over a debt and territorial dispute. Iraqi presence in Kuwait posed a potential threat to American ally Saudi Arabia. The world's eyes turned to the White House. President George H. W. Bush announced simply, "This will not stand."

President Bush began at once to assemble a coalition of thirty-four nations in an operation known as Desert Shield. With more than 500,000 American and coalition forces in place in Saudi Arabia, Bush issued an ultimatum to Saddam: Leave Kuwait by January 15, 1991, or face a full attack by the multinational force.

The January 15 deadline passed and Saddam did not budge. Bush unleashed the forces of Operation Desert Storm, and the Persian Gulf War of 1991 began the next night. It ended with Saddam's defeat forty-two days later on February 28.

Another defensive weapon is the Standard SM-2ER Block IV missile. (ER = extended range.) It is an all-weather, supersonic, ship-launched, medium-to-long-range fleet air defense missile. Also known as the RIM-156A, it provides defense for an entire fleet area. (R = surface-ship launched; IM = intercept missile.) It is deployed on destroyers and cruisers and is the latest version of the RIM-66/67 series to enter the fleet.

MIM-104 Patriot

The MIM-104 Patriot is a battlefield air-defense system. It protects against aircraft, cruise missiles, and ballistic missiles. Its mobile launcher accommodates four missiles.

Specifications
Contractor: Raytheon Systems Company
Length 17 feet 5 inches (530.86 cm)
Diameter: 1 foot 4 inches (40.64 cm)
Span (fins): 2 feet 9 inches (83.82 cm)
Weight: 1,980 pounds (898 kg)
Function: Surface-to-air
Warhead: 150 pounds (68 kg) high explosive, fragmentation
Guidance: Radar homing with radio command guidance
Status: Operational

The Patriot has undergone two upgrades known as PAC-1 and PAC-2 (Patriot Advanced Capability); the PAC-3 weapon is a complete redesign of the system.

Precision-Guided Munitions: Smart Weapons

Early in America's air campaign against the Islamic State (IS) that began in August 2014, B-1 crews from the 9th Bomb Squadron at Dyess Air Force Base, Texas, focused on a single town in Syria—Kobani. Kurdish forces known as Peshmerga were entrapped in their own city under the advance of the insurgents (Islamic State terrorists). The enemy was "sending troops there constantly," a weapons systems officer from the 9th Bomb Squadron told *Air Force Times* staff writer Brian Everstine. "They were very willing to impale themselves on that city." The fanatical terrorists were willing to die for control of the city.

Islamic State fighters moving openly on top of buildings and bridges provided plenty of targets for the airmen. The B-1 Lancer was made for missions like this one. It carried a wide variety of

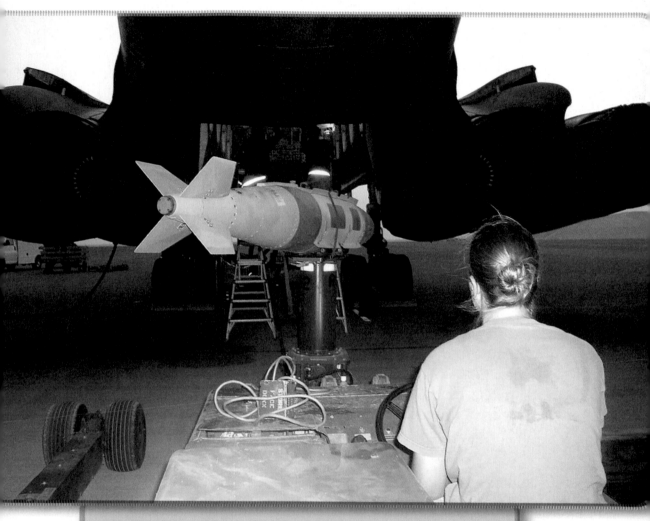

Senior Airman Tiffany Sommers positions a Guided Bomb Unit-31 Joint Direct Attack Munition for insertion in the aft bomb bay of a B-1 Lancer.

weaponry, including both general-purpose and smart bombs. Few targets can survive its destructive force. Additionally, the B-1 can stay over the target area for about ten hours without need of refueling. This loitering capability allows US airmen to react to targets supplied by Kurdish forces or develop their own targets to drive off the insurgents.

The squadron dropped an estimated 660 bombs on Kobani, killing more than a thousand IS fighters. It delivered about one-third of all the bombs dropped during the first five months of Operation Inherent Resolve, the official name of the air campaign against the Islamic State.

The 9th Bomb Squadron completed its deployment in late January 2015. By then, the Kurdish Peshmerga had secured Kobani and claimed victory. "To be part of something, to go out and stomp these guys out," said a B-1 pilot named Major Johnson, "it was completely overwhelming and exciting."

Later, Islamic State insurgents spoke to the IS-aligned news network Amak in Syria. They said the constant airstrikes forced them out of Kobani. According to CNN, one insurgent told the news agency: "I swear by God, their planes did not leave the air, day and night; they did airstrikes day and night. They targeted everything. They even attacked motorcycles; they have not left a building standing. But God willing we will return and we will have our revenge multiplied."

Kobani remains under Kurdish control.

President Barack Obama authorized the use of "smart bombs" in Iraq and Syria in the summer of 2014. By mid-March 2015, US and coalition warplanes had dropped more than 10,200 precision-guided bombs on Islamic State forces. Almost every bomb used by the United States in the air war against the Islamic State is guided by a satellite or laser. By comparison, only 10 percent of the bombs used in the Persian Gulf War in 1991 had advanced systems.

Advanced smart bombs are constructed from conventional—or "dumb"—bombs by attaching kits to them. Various conventional bombs are used to convert dumb bombs to smart bombs, including the Mk 82–84 series, the BLU-109 Penetrator, and the BLU-116 Advanced Unitary Penetrator.

B-1 Lancer

The multi-mission B-1 bomber forms the backbone of America's long-range bomber force. It carries the largest payload of both guided and unguided weapons in the air force's inventory.

Service: USAF

Armament: 84 500-pound (227 kg) Mk-82 or 24 2,000-pound (908 kg) Mk-84 general-purpose bombs; up to 84 500-pound (227 kg) Mk-62 or 8 2,000-pound (908 kg) Mk-65 Quick Strike naval mines; 30 cluster munitions (CBU-87, -89, -97) or 30 Wind-Corrected Munitions Dispensers (CBU-104, -104, -105); up to 242,000-pound (908 kg) GBU-31 or 15 500-pound (227 kg) GBU-38 Joint Direct Attack Munitions; up to 24 AGM-158A Joint Air-to-Surface Standoff Missiles; GBU-54 Laser Joint Direct Attack Munition

Power Plant: 4x General Electric F101-GE-102 turbofan engine with afterburner

Speed: 900 mph (1,448 km/h) (Mach.2 at sea level)

Range: Intercontinental

Crew: Four

A B-1 Lancer supersonic bomber takes off at Edwards Air Force Base, California.

Smart Bombs

"Precision-guided munitions" is the government phrase for smart weapons. A precision-guided munition (PGM) is a missile, bomb, or artillery shell that is fitted with a terminal guidance system. The guidance system consists of electrical equipment that guides it during its last phase before impact. In short, a smart weapon is a projectile with a homing device. PGMs are designed to precisely hit a specified target while minimizing collateral damage (unintentional death, injury, or damage).

Conventional bombs simply consist of an explosive material packed in a sturdy case with a fuse mechanism. The fuse contains a triggering device that ignites the explosive and the bomb goes off. Conventional bombs are considered "dumb" because they fall freely to the ground without any way to steer themselves. Consequently, many dumb bombs might be required to take out a single target. By contrast, smart bombs can be controlled in flight to hit the smallest target with pinpoint accuracy.

To keep pace with the daily demand for smart munitions, the US Air Force formed a special "ammo team" at the Dyess Air Force Base in Texas. Their crew of fourteen works twelve hours a day to upgrade 500- and 2,000-pound free-falling bombs to smart-bomb status. They do so by affixing a dozen parts to each "dumb" bomb—fuses, radar-equipped nose cones, GPS-guided tail fins, and more. Upgraded bombs now roll off their conveyor belt every ten minutes.

Aviation Ordnancemen unload a laser-guided bomb from the wing of an F/A-18C on the flight deck of the Nimitz-class aircraft carrier USS *Carl Vinson*. The ship conducts flight operations in the US 5th Fleet area of responsibility supporting Operation Inherent Resolve.

FACT

Guidance Systems

Smart bombs currently used by US forces rely on two basic guidance systems—laser and Global Positioning System (GPS).

Laser

Laser-guided bombs (LGBs) remain the most numerous precision-guided munition with some twenty-five thousand in the US inventory. The system relies on a target designator on the ground or in an aircraft illuminating the target with a laser beam. The laser beam is reflected off the target. When the LGB is released, it locks on to the beam it has been programmed to search for and follows it to the target.

GPS

The bomb's GPS receiver pinpoints a particular target on the ground. Before release of the bomb, the aircraft's computer feeds the bomb's computer its current position and the GPS coordinates of the target. In flight, the bomb's GPS receiver processes signals from the GPS satellite to keep on track to the target. The bomb doesn't have to see a thing to find its way to the target.

Nuclear Deterrence: Missileers and Missile Sites

"**A**s a Nuclear and Missile Operations Officer, you will effectively and efficiently operate and manage nuclear and missile operations systems to defend and support the United States and allied forces." So begins the US Air Force career description for the officers entrusted with the last line of defense of the United States—and ultimately with the fate of the world.

Since the 1960s, a small group of air force personnel known as missileers has been working in a shadowy world deep underground at America's launch control centers, responsible for 450 Minuteman III missiles. Missileers remain vigilant 24/7, ready to act at once on the president's order—an order they hope will never come. Their unique job allows no room for error. It demands efficiency, focus, and constant operational alertness. To meet the uncommon

First Lieutenant Brittany Morton, left, and her missileer partner answer their phones during a trainer ride at the missile procedures trainer. Two missileers man a launch control center and take turns sleeping.

physical and mental demands of their responsibilities, missileers must undergo rigorous initial and recurrent training.

Missile Combat Crews

Future managers of America's Minuteman III ICBM system receive operational readiness training at Vandenberg Air Force Base (AFB). The base is located on the central coast of California between the towns of Lompoc and Santa Maria. Training is conducted by the 532nd Training Squadron of the 381st Training Group.

A team of US Air Force Global Strike Command airmen conduct an operational test launch of an unarmed Minuteman III intercontinental ballistic missile from Vandenberg Air Force Base. Test launches are used to verify the accuracy and reliability of the ICBM weapon system, providing valuable data to ensure a safe, secure, and effective nuclear deterrent.

FACT

Minuteman III ICBM
Launch Sites

The current Minuteman force is divided into three missile wings, each consisting of a wing staff and five groups: operations, maintenance, support, security, and medical. Each wing operates 150 Minuteman III ICBMs on full alert 24/7, 365 days a year. The three wings are located at:

Francis E. Warren AFB, Wyoming: Located about 3 miles (5 km) west of Cheyenne, it houses the Twentieth Air Force and the 90th Missile Wing. The wing's stated mission is to defend America with the world's premier combat-ready ICBM force.

Malmstrom AFB, Montana: Home to the 341st Missile Wing, the base is located near Great Falls, Montana. The wing pledges to defend America with safe, secure, effective nuclear forces and combat-ready Airmen.

Minot AFB, North Dakota: Situated 13 miles (21 km) north of the city of Minot, it is the only AFB housing two arms of the US nuclear triad: the 91st Missile Wing and the 5th Bomb Wing (B-52H Stratofortress bombers). The 91st vows to defend the United States with safe, secure, and effective ICBMs in support of the president and combatant commands.

All three wings form a part of the Twentieth Air Force, which in turn reports to the Air Force Global Strike Command (AFGSC), headquartered at Barksdale AFB, Louisiana.

Initial and advanced training is provided in three phases: initial qualification training, unit qualification training, and recurrent training. Trainees are taught ICBM operations and procedures and are trained as electronic, electro- and missile-mechanical, and facility maintenance technicians.

After six months of initial qualification training, the new missileers are assigned to missile combat crews at one of three Minuteman III sites, where they continue unit training. Thereafter, crews undergo training and evaluation once or twice a month to ensure their skills remain razor sharp. Monthly training consists of about two days of classroom training, covering such things as emergency war orders, weapons systems operations, and code controls. Periodic competitions are also held with other crews to instill pride of unit and vie for top honors.

Changing the Guard

A typical day for two launch control officers of the oncoming watch at Minot AFB begins on an elevator that takes them dozens of feet underground. They exit at the bottom of the elevator shaft and step into a netherworldly, bottom-of-the-world atmosphere.

Proceeding through a sealed, 8-ton [8.82 tonne], 2-foot-thick [.61-m] concrete blast door, they arrive at the Launch Control Center (LCC). The LCC is called "the capsule" because its shape resembles a pill. It is suspended in air by four king-sized shock absorbers. A second blast door seals its entrance. The new watch officers announce their arrival, and the door swings open. They are greeted by the old watch officers and enter the capsule. Crammed with green and white computer equipment, the capsule's tight interior speaks to the high-tech nature of the nation's work being conducted there.

LCC procedures require the old and new launch commanders to conduct a detailed inspection of the entire capsule and all its equipment. Together, they verify that everything is in order and all

In preparation for an unarmed Minuteman III missile launch, 1st Lieutenant Kimberly Erskine practices procedures at Vandenberg Air Force Base.

the equipment is working properly. After a satisfactory inspection, the incoming commander signs a form attesting to a satisfactory inspection and takes command of the LCC. For the next twenty-four hours, he and his deputy will remain in charge of the LCC and ten Minuteman III ICBMs that are dispersed about the North Dakota countryside in strategic locations. Above ground, in their support, a team of airmen stands by to provide security and food and to ensure that all equipment remains in working order.

LGM-30 Minuteman III

The LGM-30 Minuteman III is the longest-serving intercontinental ballistic missile—and arguably the most important offensive missile system—in America's weapons arsenal. It replaces the earlier Atlas and Titan. The LGM-30 was itself replaced in part by the LGM-118 Peacekeeper, or MX, missile, but then replaced its replacement, primarily due to cost considerations.

Specifications
Function: Surface-to-surface ICBM
Contractor: Boeing
Length: 59 feet 10 inches (17.98 m)
Diameter: 5 feet 6 inches (167.64 cm)
Weight: 79,432 pounds (36,063 kg)
Guidance: Inertial
Warhead: W87 Nuclear Warhead, 330 KT
Users: US Air Force
Status: Operational

Sergeant Stephen M. Kravitsky inspects an LGM-30 Minuteman III missile inside a silo.

The commander and his deputy necessarily sit for hours at their launch control panels. They often trade places while the partner rests. But each launch officer remains ever aware of the enormous power at his or her hand: One toggle switch can send a single nuclear warhead—with twenty times the explosive force of the first atom bomb—hurtling across the globe at speeds of 15,000 mph (24,140 km/hr).

At the end of their twenty-four-hour alert, another set of missileers arrives to relieve them. They greet the newcomers just as they were greeted before. And they leave the cramped capsule to await their next alert, thankful for yet another watch without incident. In more than fifty years, Minuteman missileers have never had to launch a live missile, but they stand eternally on guard—America's silent sentinels.

TIMELINE

1944—Unmanned V-1 and V-2 rockets bomb Great Britain during World War II.

1957—Soviets shock the world with the launch of *Sputnik I*; Americans launch the Atlas intercontinental ballistic missile.

1958—Americans launch the *Explorer I* satellite with a Redstone missile.

1959—Titan I missile takes to the air.

1962—US U-2F aircraft spots a Soviet ballistic missile in western Cuba, inciting the Cuban Missile Crisis.

1965—Atlas and Titan I missiles are replaced by Titan II and Minuteman I missiles.

1974—Minuteman I missiles are replaced by Minuteman II and Minuteman III missiles.

1982—US Air Force deactivates Titan II missiles.

1999—Minuteman II missiles are phased out and replaced by Minuteman III missiles.

2003—US cruise missiles strike Baghdad at start of the Iraq War.

2010—The future Islamic State under Abu Bakr al-Baghdadi arises from the remnants of al-Qaeda in Iraq.

2014—President Obama orders air strikes against the Islamic State in August.

ballistic missile—A missile (rocket) that follows a high-arch trajectory to deliver one or more warheads to a designated target.

bomb—A container filled with explosive or incendiary material set off by impact or a timing device.

GPS—A navigational system that transmits radio signals from twenty-four Earth-orbiting satellites, giving the location of each satellite and the time of the transmission.

insurgent—One who rises in revolt against civil authority or an established government; a rebel.

missile—An object or weapon suitable for throwing or projecting at a target.

Mutually Assured Destruction (MAD)—A defense policy assuring no nuclear power would attack another, for it would mean certain death for both.

nuclear energy—Energy that is released or absorbed during reactions taking place in the nuclei of atoms.

Operation Paperclip—The secret intelligence program that brought Nazi scientists to America late in World War II and thereafter.

propellant—An agent, such as fuel, that provides thrust for a rocket.

reconnaissance—An exploration or examination of an area in order to obtain information about it, especially for military purposes.

turbofan engine—A type of aircraft jet engine based on a gas turbine that generates thrust by using a combination of a ducted fan and a jet exhaust nozzle. It passes part of the air from the ducted fan through the core, which provides oxygen to burn fuel to create power.

unmanned aircraft systems operator—Remote pilots of unmanned aircraft that gather intelligence.

FURTHER READING

BOOKS

Dougherty, Martin. *The Most Amazing Weapons of War.* North Mankato, MN: Capstone Publishers, 2010.

Freese, Susan M. *Nuclear Weapons.* Edina, MN: Abdo Publishing, 2011.

Gagne, Tammy. *Incredible Military Weapons*. Edina, MN: Abdo Publishing, 2015.

Nardo, Don. *In the Air: Missiles*. Greensboro, NC: Morgan Reynolds Publishing, 2014.

Senker, Cath. *Kennedy and the Cuban Missile Crisis*. North Mankato, MN: Heinemann-Raintree, 2014.

WEBSITES

The History Learning Site

historylearningsite.co.uk/world-war-two/world-war-two-in-western-europe/the-v-revenge-weapons/the-v1

Here is the story of Germany's V-1 flying bomb.

Social Studies for Kids

socialstudiesforkids.com/articles/ushistory/cubanmissilecrisis1.htm

Read about the Cold War and the Cuban Missile Crisis.

US Air Force

af.mil/News/ArticleDisplay/tabid/223/Article/585408/missile-alert-facility-life-60-feet-under.aspx

Learn about the missile alert facility, 60 feet (18 m) below ground.